Presented To

my precious Kathy

By

Gayle Roberson

9/9/12

Endorsements

"*I highly recommend this book by an expert on compassion and disrupted lives. Over the years he has touched countless lives and faced the really tough questions, and it shows in this book. You will be moved from tears to laughter.*"

—**Dr. Paul Faulkner**, counselor and author of *Making Things Right When Things Go Wrong*

"*Virgil Fry has written a sensitive and helpful book. It will be useful to chaplains, ministers, counselors, and people going through the fear, disruption, and grief of their own illness or that of someone close to them. Virgil mixes short and often poignant reflections with poetic words on the reality of God. He raises questions and points to new meanings that may be encountered in the unexpected and ticketless journey of illness. This book will speak to a lot of people.*"

—**Keith Miller**, author of *A Taste of New Wine and The Secret Life of the Soul*

"*I find this book helpful to all, and especially to my health care provider colleagues. We often need help before we can help others. Dr. Fry is to be commended for taking us along on his journey in ministering to patients, families, and health providers over the past many years—we can all gain from his experience to find help in handling life's disrupting experiences.*"

—**Dr. Roger W. Anderson** former Director, Division of Pharmacy, University of Texas M. D. Anderson Cancer Center

"*Drawing on years of experience, Dr. Fry eloquently describes the great emotional and spiritual challenges encountered by those committed to the care of the seriously ill and their families. His insights show that there are ways to find purpose, meaning, and hope in the face of life-threatening illness.*"

—**Dr. Alan D. Valentine**, Department of Psychiatry, University of Texas
   M. D. Anderson Cancer Center

"*We experienced disruption firsthand—a strange city, an unfamiliar hospital, a son newly diagnosed with leukemia. It was in this nightmare that we came to know Virgil. Through this book, you too will come to know his insight, faith, and compassion.*"

—**Glenn and Mary Stinchcomb**, Oklahoma City

Disrupted

FINDING GOD IN ILLNESS AND LOSS

VIRGIL M. FRY

LEAFWOOD
PUBLISHERS
Abilene, TX

Disrupted: FINDING GOD IN ILLNESS AND LOSS

LEAFWOOD
PUBLISHERS

Copyright 1999, 2007 by Virgil M. Fry

ISBN 0-89112-516-7

Printed in the United States of America

Unless otherwise indicated, biblical quotations are from the Holy Bible, New International Version (NIV), Copyright © 1973, 1978, 1984 by International Bible Society. Other versions used: New American Standard Bible (NASB) Copyright © The Lockman Foundation, 1960, 1962, 1963, 1971, 1972, 1973, 1975, 1977; Today's English Version (TEV), Copyright © Thomas Nelson, 1993; Contemporary English Version (CEV), Copyright © Thomas Nelson, 1996.

Cover design by Greg Jackson; interior design by Mark Decker

For information contact:
Leafwood Publishers, Abilene, Texas
1-877-816-4455 toll free
www.leafwoodpublishers.com

07 08 09 10 11 12 / 7 6 5 4 3 2 1

Dedication

To Caryl,
a true gift from God

Acknowledgments

This book, originally published by 21st Century Christian, is now updated as a companion book to *Rekindled: Warmed by Fires of Hope* (Leafwood). Both books spring from the medical world of patients, families, and medical staff who allow me to journey alongside them as a chaplain and a companion.

This work emanates from the ministry of Lifeline Chaplaincy, an organization whose mission is to reflect a God of love and service to the seriously ill and grieving (www.lifelinechaplaincy.org). I am blessed to be associated with such a marvelous group of caring people. The strength I feel from their support is truly unconditional and wonderful...indeed, a gift from God.

So many have helped refine and produce this book that I cannot mention them all. The response of readers across the country, many of whom have written warm, gracious notes of gratitude, is a blessing to me. I also am extremely grateful to the joy of my life: my family Caryl, Kyle, and Kacie, to my extended family, and to a host of friends who are also family to me.

Thanks to all who make this book possible, including Barry Brewer and Leonard Allen, and to God for broadening this chaplain's daily workplace into an audience of spiritual seekers everywhere.

Contents

Section Three

Section Four

Section Five

Preface

Illness and loss affects everyone. Like it or not, we are mortal. We experience disruptions. And these disruptions teach us.

This book invites you into my world. Since 1985 I have been ministering in the world-renowned University of Texas M. D. Anderson Cancer Center in Houston, Texas. Through my years of walking up and down hospital corridors and crisscrossing clinic stations, I have been deeply impacted. In walking beside those on the road of cancer survival, I have learned much about love, priorities, and tenacity. The saying is true: in serving others you are yourself served.

This book uses the biblical imagery of journeying through a variety of landscapes. You may read the book in its entirety or in snippets, focusing on the section closest to your current experience. The content is laid out to address specific points of your journey:

Stormy Seas—When Health Is Threatened
In the Wilderness—When Answers Aren't Clear
Sharing the Trail—Being a Caregiver
In the Valley of the Shadow—When Grief and Loss Prevail
Green Pastures—Times of Reflection and Thanksgiving

My prayerful hope is that these reflections will enrich and better equip you for your spiritual journey. And may the God of us all be thanked for eternal promises to supply everything we need on that path.

Virgil M. Fry

When a Chaplain Needs a Chaplain

It's different once you have been there

"We've ordered an ambulance. We're going to transfer Kyle to Texas Children's Hospital. They'll be here within 30 minutes."

The doctor's words shocked us. Surely there must be some mistake. Our 13-year-old son couldn't be the one needing to be transferred from our community hospital to a pediatric acute care center.

We had already spent a week anticipating a diagnosis. His abdominal cramps and bloody diarrhea had continued unabated. A severe drop in platelet count and a rise in creatinine level indicated more trouble. Microscopic bacteria had ravaged the colon; the kidneys were next. Without dialysis, my son's life was on the line.

The next two weeks were a blur: a week in intensive care... six dialysis treatments... blood transfusions... nothing to eat or drink... swollen limbs and shocked system. In just a matter of days, Kyle's life was transformed from typical teenager to one fighting for survival.

The end of the story is a good one. A month passed, and Kyle was able to attend camp for a boys' choir. His body, though weakened at the time, has returned to normalcy. As this book goes to press, he is a newlywed, a band director, and one who is full of hopes, dreams, and thanksgiving.

So how does this experience impact his mother, sister, extended family, friends, and me? In numerous ways, some of which are still being processed. The shocking numbness of crisis has slowly given way to reflection, to returning to living purposefully. The line between good health and serious illness is a thin one, one easily crossed in the briefest of time.

One Saturday evening ICU visiting hours were closed. Caryl and I went to a restaurant for supper. We looked at the people around us, wondering what their day had been like without the overshadowing concern of a sick child. We wondered how often we had been blithely oblivious to someone else's burden while we scurried about our daily business. We were reminded: life is precious, and health is a gift that is too often considered a right.

Supportive care takes on special significance when you are on the receiving end. When feeling overwhelmed by disruptive news about your child, you cherish those who respond with open arms. Your heart replays the words, "You are in our prayers." You marvel at the therapeutic catharsis that transpires when the words "I love you" aren't minced. You find that God's presence is made tangible in the voices and hands of His children.

Sometimes it's not easy being a chaplain at a cancer center. It is harder, however, being a family member of a seriously ill patient. More than ever, I appreciate the words of Jesus: I was sick, and you visited me. Such words confirm that the Lord of Heaven identifies Himself with hurting humanity.

This is truly Good News.

Disrupted

SECTION ONE:

Stormy Seas
When Health Is Threatened

Stormy Seas

When Health Is Threatened

"Water, water everywhere...

nor any drop to drink."

This is how Samuel Taylor Coleridge paints the picture of the desolate, sea-stranded sailor. Readers of *Rime of the Ancient Mariner* sense the irony: life-saving water at times becomes life-threatening.

The Bible abounds with water and sea imagery. Separating bodies of water from land is one of the first orders of the creation narrative. And ever since, humanity has sought a balance between dependence upon and fearful awe of seas.

Geographically and spiritually, seas have the capacity to disrupt and destroy. My wife and I once rode a ship across the Sea of Galilee. At the trip's midpoint, a fellow-passenger read the story of Jesus being summoned by frightened disciples to speak a word of peace. The same sea, which we enjoyed that beautiful day, was seen as the epitome of chaos by the disciples.

Few events are more sea-churning than serious illness. Health is usually relegated to the realm of expected privilege—until it is threatened. When we face potentially catastrophic disease, we quickly identify with those who cling to life aboard easily tossed ships. At such times, we feel disoriented and rudderless, looking for a place to anchor ourselves.

Summoning God to speak a word of peace—what a blessing, when we are confronted with stormy seas.

Heal me, O Lord,
and I will be healed;
save me and I will be saved,
for You are the One I praise.

Jeremiah 17:14

Stormy Seas

A Prayer of the Sick

Lord,

You have promised us Your presence.
I feel the need of that presence now for comfort,
for strength.

My illness saps my energy.
The unknown disrupts my routine.
My family and friends are hurting too.
Sometimes the anxiety is too much.
Sometimes You seem distant.
Sometimes I hurt in loneliness.

Father, heal my spirit and my body.
Walk with me.
Assure me that You are here.
Remind me that Your grace is sufficient.

Be with those who care for me.
Help me to care for them as well.
Remember my fellow-sufferers.
In Your grace and love, remember us all.

For being here with me, thank You.
Through Jesus the Christ,

Amen.

You cannot prevent the birds of
sorrow from flying over your head,
but you can prevent them from
building nests in your hair.

—Chinese proverb

Stormy Seas

Facing Serious Illness

Adjust to new limitations without becoming passive.

Love and be loved.

Remind yourself: no one is an island.

Pray fervently. Be honest and specific.

Educate yourself about treatment.

Maintain hope, dignity, and purpose.

Allow feelings to be expressed. Remember: Jesus wept.

Feed yourself with the Living Bread.

Meditate. Let your mind work with your body.

Receive the support offered by caring people.

Remember we can only live one day at a time.

Claim the gift of God's presence.

Happiness is not a state at
which to arrive,
but a manner of traveling.

—Margaret Lee Runbeck

Stormy Seas

HOSPITAL BLANKETS AND PICNIC BASKETS

Mike was pensive, and more than a little homesick for Tennessee. In a Houston hospital room for five months of cancer treatments, this 26-year-old newlywed was sick of being sick. His thoughts were saturated with getting on with living, not merely surviving.

The room was dark. He spoke in hushed tones, as if to keep check on his tumultuous frustrations. We talked of home, marriage, basketball, shortened life expectancy, careers, God and church.

Feeling the heaviness of our conversation, I pointedly asked Mike: "If you were back home today, what would you want to do?"

Without hesitation he answered, "Go on a picnic." He continued, "I'd get my wife, we'd pack some great tasting food and a blanket, and head for the hills. Then we'd simply enjoy the day and each other."

Playing devil's advocate, I said, "What about ants?"

He countered with a grin. "Let them come along. They're not capable of ruining my picnic!"

We laughed. Consider the absurdity of having a fantasy picnic marred by tiny six-legged invaders. In the midst of weighing life versus death issues, ants are virtually powerless to ruin any good event.

I learned something that day. He could have stated his desire to work for some grand humanitarian project. Instead, his wish was for time to reconnect with life by way of an ordinary-sounding picnic.

I learned again that deep reflective wrestling is not just centered on so-called spiritual matters. God's loving-kindness is as evident in simple picnics as in the greatest of altruistic endeavors. To allow the fear of ants to rob us of the joy of a picnic is to rob ourselves of an encounter with God.

A few weeks before his death, Mike was able to go on several picnics. Funny, he never once complained about ants. He was too overwhelmed with a sense of gratitude to notice.

Bring on the ants. A lot of picnics are waiting for us.

Disrupted

Mirth is the sweet wine
of human life.
It should be offered sparkling
with zestful life unto God.

—Henry Ward Beecher

OOPS! (STATEMENTS YOU'D RATHER NOT HEAR FROM YOUR DOCTOR OR NURSE)

"Hmmmmm...this is the first time that's ever happened!"

"This may sting a little."

"Wouldn't you know it—that vein collapsed!"

"We'd like to run a few more tests."

"Hold still."

"Please lie down on this stainless steel table."

"Let me put some gloves on."

"You can change into this robe now."

"We keep it cold in here to prevent infection."

"Turn your head and cough!"

"Do you have a will?"

"The office can work out a payment plan."

"Are you a religious person?"

"I'll be back in a few minutes."

"You need to sign a few papers first."

"We don't file insurance or Medicare."

"OOPS!"

There must be more to life
than having everything.

—Maurice Sendak

Stormy Seas

Lessons Gleaned While Standing Beside the Sick

Hope is stronger than despair,
though both are powerful and normal.

Being avoided or shunned is worse than being
subjected to uncomfortable conversation.

Life is seldom fair, objective, or predictable
in spite of our efforts to make it so.

The message "life goes on" takes on deeper meanings
as we confront crisis.

Waiting, being quiet, and receiving is more difficult
than doing, talking, and giving.

Busy schedules do not silence inner struggles, but do
mask hidden emotions that beg to be shared.

Loss of independence is a loss of identity,
for we perceive ourselves as doers and actors.

Losses painfully remind us of how dependent
we truly are upon God and others.

A broken spirit can be more difficult to heal
than a broken body.

When we have to, we can endure much more than we
think we can. The human spirit is incredibly resilient.

Claiming one day at a time
is one secret to faithful living.

The most important things in life cannot be bought
or earned, but they can be received in love.

Time flies whether you're sick or healthy—
days quickly turn into weeks, months, and years.

Sharing sorrows and joys
yields a return of healing and intimacy.

We humans spend a great deal of time
assuming we'll live forever—we're always shocked
when we recognize our mortality.

The comfort of knowing that God is the same yesterday,
today and tomorrow is inexpressible in times of turmoil.

Faith, hope, and love are the keys to confronting unex-
plainable mysteries.

Living is a process, not a series of rational decisions
we make. Spiritual growth springs from continually
learning to "let go and let God."

Stormy Seas

The more serious the illness, the more important it is for you to fight back, mobilizing all your resources—spiritual, emotional, intellectual, physical.

—Norman Cousins

Stormy Seas

PRAYER FOR MEDICAL PERSONNEL

Lord God,

Thank you for those whose vocation is medical care. Working with the tools of Your handiwork, they manipulate all available means to counter the surge of sickness and trauma.

Wearing white coats, nurses' uniforms, or scrubs, they appear at my side. Utilizing charts and tests and years of training, they listen to my body's voices and stories. My trust level increases as I sense their technological skills and their regard for my worth.

At times, Lord, they get so caught up in the inner working of the body they forget that people are much more than parts of a machine. At times they get so immersed in the struggles of their patients that they find themselves discouraged and overwhelmed.

They, like me, wrestle with the limitations of humanity...with the incredibly disruptive capabilities of microscopic bacteria and viruses...with the violent damage inflicted by accidents and fellow human beings...with the unfairness of seeing children's innocence snatched away by heartbreaking realities.

God, forgive the times they forget that this is Your world. Likewise, forgive the times I expect them to be You.

Bless them, Lord. May they be guided by the wisdom of You, the Great Physician. May they find fulfillment through investment of themselves in the care of others. May they continue to learn skill, patience, and worth for all Your creation. Bless their families who adjust schedules to accommodate the needs of others.

Lord God, Thank you for those whose vocation is medical care.

Through the name of the Ultimate Healer,

Amen.

Disrupted

Stormy Seas

Overwhelmed

He knows not his own strength
that hath not met adversity.

—Ben Johnson

Lord God,
It's one of those days.
The kind where everything surges, leaving me overwhelmed.
The kind I try to avoid, try to suppress, try to muster my energy to fight back.
But somehow, today it's not working.

When others ask how I am, I answer, "Fine."
When they question my aloofness, I smile.
When they push for honesty, I hesitate.
When they express concern, I thank them.

Why is it Lord, that there are days like this?
Do I dare ask? Do I really want to know?

In my mind's eye, I rehearse other overwhelmed strugglers.
Like Moses, fed up with exasperating fellow wanderers.
Like Hannah, praying so earnestly that she was deemed drunk.

Like Jeremiah, lamenting the cruel fate of his people.
Like Mary, stung by unclear words of her 12-year-old.

Such stories, in a powerful way, confront and comfort me.
They remind me again that my view is, at best, partial…
That my story, like everyone's story, is ongoing and unfolding…
That paradoxically, being overwhelmed and insecure can be a statement of faith…
That such days serve as a corrective balance to overbooked schedules that fail to reflect on Your handiwork.

Lord, it is good to be alive, sustained by Your Spirit, cognizant of Your mercy, justice and love.
For the times You restore my soul, with or without my prayer to do so,
I stand truly grateful and amazed.

May Your creation forever proclaim Your caring ways.

Amen.

SECTION TWO

In the Wilderness
When Answers Aren't Clear

In the Wilderness—
When Answers Aren't Clear

The journey towards completion and fulfillment is another way of describing spirituality. Each of us possesses a drive that our spirits experience as uncertainty and anguish. From a biblical perspective, this inner chaos propels us in the direction of our Creator.

God thus appears as One far removed from simple, formulaic equations. The Bible, even when it mentions commandments, portrays the Lord as a personal God. It is no small matter when our theology is shaped by such a God: One whose very image we reflect. This is a God who, in every sense, knows us, calls us, redeems us, accepts us, loves us. For the Christian, nothing compares to the unfolding narrative of the incarnation: God becoming flesh in the form of Jesus.

Our lives on planet Earth are touched and molded by this God who understands. We seek order and predictability in structuring our lives; instead, we encounter chaos and disorder.

It is at the juncture of entering life's unpredictable arenas that we sometimes wander, as the ancient Israelites did in the wilderness. For reasons we cannot always know, we are called to launch out in faith for destinations that we haven't seen. And quite frequently, we question, cry out, get discouraged, and wonder why.

The name Israel literally means "one who wrestles with God." What a fascinating concept, for seekers of the Lord to be named wrestlers. But it's right there in the story of Jacob and the angel of God (Genesis 32:28).

So when we are in the wilderness times, wrestling with our circumstances and perhaps even with God, we are in the greatest of company. From Adam and Eve to Abraham and Sarah to David and the prophets to Jesus and the disciples—the wilderness is considered a vital component of spiritual growth.

We don't have to enjoy suffering, or to seek it, or to stoically endure it, in order to be considered faithful. We just have to go through it, knowing the wilderness never has the last word.

Keine Antwort ist auch eine Antwort.

(No answer is also an answer.)

—German proverb

In the Wilderness

WHY DO YOU ASK?

20-year-old surviving daughter: "The world is full of bad people. Why did my mother, a good woman, have to die so young?"

50-year-old man in recovery: "I'm an electrician by trade. Would someone tell me how I'm supposed to do my work with one arm surgically removed?"

35-year old terminal melanoma patient: "Sometimes I wonder about my prayers. Does God hear me when I continually present my wish list? Does He expect me to pray in a less selfish way?"

Questions. Hard questions! Questions that reflect pierced hearts... Unanswerable questions of faith and doubt... Questions trying to make sense of the incomprehensible.

Are such questions wrong? Often the question-asker thinks so. Often questions like these are asked tentatively, almost expecting lightening bolts of displeasure.

Sometimes the questions are stated as fact. Yet, they are questions just the same. "I know God must have a reason for this." "I know we're not supposed to ask why." "I wonder where God is in all of this."

Questions are not without biblical precedent. Questions of David, Job, prophets, apostles, and crowds permeate the pages of biblical narratives.

The Lord is also presented as a questioner. Which of us cannot feel the sting of God's questions in Eden: "Where are you hiding, Adam and Eve?" Or the haunting cry of the merciful wounded God in Hosea 11: "How can I give you up, O Israel?"

Jesus' teachings were peppered with questions that invited people to consider the answer within themselves. "Whose face is on the coin?" "Who was the true neighbor?" "Do you see these stones?" "When the Son of Man returns, will he find faith on earth?"

God utilizes questions to ponder aloud.... To reveal inner turmoil...To correct in kindness...To call His children to drink more deeply of spiritual waters.

Thus a questioning spirit seems to reflect our created nature. Curiosity is innate within us. God wants us to act upon our curiosity. It's a matter of trusting in His all-powerful goodness.

Do the questions that defy easy answers offend God? Hardly. We don't surprise God with our honesty. We only fool ourselves if we try to soft-pedal our innermost thoughts and feelings.

Is it a sign of weakness to question God? No. Such questioning is based on faith—faith that has been shaken, but still faith. God invites us to share our experiences—joyful and painful. Growth is nurtured in such exchanges.

Verbalizing questions helps us enter into holy ground, seeking God's own heart. Perhaps we should take our cue from children who seldom hesitate to ask. "Why did God create snakes, mosquitoes, and homework?" "When was God born?" "Why do people get sick and die?" "Why is there war?"

We adults who fumble with pat answers for these questions would be wise to say, "I don't know, but I'd sure like to know!" God doesn't need us to defend Him. He can provide His own defense. Scriptures tell us: Ask the tough questions. God understands the deep feelings behind them. After all, God is "One acquainted with grief."

Questions. We hear them all the time. Maybe we need to give ourselves permission to ask our own questions. God invites us to be more than spectators in our walk of faith. He invites us to ponder aloud...To reveal inner turmoil...To correct in kindness...To join others in drinking more deeply of spiritual waters.

Will we?

Kind looks, kind words, kind acts,
and warm handshakes—these
are secondary means of grace
when men are in trouble and are
fighting their unseen battles.

—John Hall

In the Wilderness

DAMAGED GOODS, BROKEN COOKIES, AND THUMBS

"Sometimes I feel like damaged goods." The statement came from a nice-looking, highly successful woman. She's witty, energetic, and smart. She's been praised for being a model teacher, church member, mother, and spouse.

And yet, few people ever know of her struggle to fit in. Now middle-aged, she's been diabetic since age 5. Daily injections, blood and urine testing, and monitoring food intake aren't flashy conversation topics for a child or adult. This disease is not one that shows, but when it is known, advice like "Is that on your diet?" flows freely.

That's where the rub comes: at times, to her it seems like the whole world is healthy and happy, and that she's taking care of business alone.

Yet, it's that inner battle that sensitizes her to others. She's a master at tuning in to the hidden messages of fellow strugglers who also feel like damaged goods.

At Camp Star Trails for children and siblings living with cancer, they sing a wonderful song by Larry Penn:

> I'm a Little Cookie, yes I am,
> I was made by the cookie man

On my way from the cookie pan
A little piece broke off a me.

A little piece broke off a me, uh humm
A little piece broke off a me, uh humm
But I can taste just as good, uh humm,
As a regular cookie can.

Now I ain't as round as I might be,
But I'll taste good, just wait and see,
And I can love back just twice as hard
As any regular cookie can. ©

There are many experiences that can cause us to perceive ourselves as less-than-perfect. All of us struggle with inner turmoil fostered by unseen elements: depression, hidden temptations and passions, relational rifts, alienation from God and humanity, evil motives, violated trusts.

Many years ago Dr. Paul Faulkner preached a sermon on thumbs that I'll never forget. He held up his hand and pointed to four long fingers that look similar, as if they are part of a matched set. In comparison, he held up his thumb. Shorter, off-centered, not quite like the others, the thumb can definitely suffer from an inferiority complex. But it's the thumb that truly gives power and dexterity to the other fingers. Try to tie your shoes without your thumb!

In human terms, we all feel like thumbs in certain areas. As if everyone else is percolating along without a care in the world. As if no one can grasp or is willing to listen to our stories of brokenness and limitations. But in reality we, like the oddball thumb, are a vital part of teams that cannot function without us.

In those moments when we view ourselves as damaged goods, broken cookies, and thumbs, opportunity is given to hear higher, deeper callings. Voices from the past break through the centuries and proclaim:

A bruised reed He will not destroy.
(Isaiah 42:3)

Come to me, all you who are weary and burdened,
and I will give you rest.
(Matthew 11:28)

Lord God, we are mindful of our need for rest, refreshment, and restitution. We are aware of our broken spirits, and we believe in Your promise to make us whole. Help us, Lord, to use our brokenness as a bridge to You, and as a bridge to others around us who also feel like damaged goods. Through the One who loves us into wholeness.

Amen.

Sometimes I get the feeling
that the whole world
is against me, but deep down
I know that's not true.

Some of the smaller
countries are neutral.

—Robert Orben

In the Wilderness

CHANGE: IS IT ALL IT'S CRACKED UP TO BE?

Who hasn't said that in the middle of change: "The world is against me. It's too much." Seeking solace, we long for the way it used to be, when the world was simpler and more manageable. And then we remember that our rose-colored memories can be selective, seeing yesteryears as the good old days.

Transitioning to a new century forcefully reminds us of the homespun axiom, "The only thing that stays the same is change." Americans have literally gone from space traveling dreamers to moon walkers. Rather than having a horse tied to a post, we have tethered ourselves to beepers, faxes, computers and cell phones.

Working in a large medical complex confirms further that change is everywhere. The world of healthcare is always in flux. Massive buildings replace existing ones, nurses are in short supply, insurance coverage changes daily, and new tests and treatments come forth constantly. Patients, families, and staff will testify from firsthand anecdotes: things are not the same.

Change is at the core of life. Every organism, from smallest microbe to largest mammal, is caught up in change. Movement processing toward something else is tantamount to being alive. When an organism stops moving, life ceases.

Yet, we humans have a need to anchor to something for stability. We find ourselves pulled by the poles of finite limitations and infinite expansiveness. When our world changes too rapidly for our own comfort, we become anxious. We grieve over losses. We wax nostalgic. We petition God, hoping to avoid the ambivalent feelings which might include painful change. We stay busy, failing to reflect upon and fully feel our losses.

And then we look at Scripture. Change and change agents play a particularly important role to the Lord. The dialectical tension of chaos and order begins with Genesis 1 and weaves all the way through Revelation 22.

People of faith have always had to cope with change, all the while seeking to find purpose and meaning therein.

Hebrew instructors like the Psalmists exhorted their people to remember: to retell stories of captivity, wanderings, and freedom and to revisit through the mind's eye the sites of failure and forgiveness. Christian texts also call for remembrance, coupled with awe and thanksgiving. In such events, a message of promised Presence is heralded—a message even louder than the noise of change.

For those who refuse to accept change, life can be especially burdensome. When God set a table filled with an offensive menu, Peter found his initial response to change was an instant, emphatic, "No, Lord!" (Acts 10). Hosea laments for his fellow citizens: "Israel has a chance to live, but is too foolish to take it—like a child about to be born, who refuses to come out of the womb" (13:13 TEV).

So how do we respond in a way that is faithful to how God would have us to be? With an occasional trip down memory lane. With a heart that feels the heaviness of losses. With a mind that refuses to stop growing and learning.

With a spirit of willingness to trust in God's loving-kindness, even if we don't know the whole story.

And then we move on, experiencing life in more meaningful ways than we ever dreamed possible. We launch out into the deep.

Thank God, there are times when our comfort level is shaken, forcing us to come out of the womb.

God

Alone

Understands

—From the gravemarker
of a mother who left behind five children

In the Wilderness

SEEING BEYOND THE CHAOS

Sometimes I struggle within myself, trying to make sense of the chaos within the hospital where I work. Where is a hopeful word when everyone seems to be overwhelmed by distressing circumstance? Circumstances such as:

A 41-year-old husband and father of three being sent home to die after being diagnosed two months ago.

A newly diagnosed 19-year-old who begins her chemotherapy regimen only a week after being told she has lymphoma.

A 20-year-old college student who had to interrupt his university studies because of a recurring brain tumor with few medical options left.

A hospital employee who came to my office in tears because her 16-year-old alcoholic nephew is dominating the lives of her and her two children.

This list is but the tip of the proverbial iceberg.

Chaos runs rampant, not only in this place, but everywhere humanity exists. Check today's headlines of lawsuits and violence. Listen to reports of company downsizing, church splits, and civil wars. The fairy tale phrase "and they lived happily ever after" becomes fodder for cynicism.

So where's the hopeful word? The comforting phrase? The snappy answer?

Perhaps my focus is skewed when it's focused solely on people. We humans are, after all, only a part of creation, not the whole. Distressing news can serve as a reminder: We need a loving Power that transcends our chaos.

The ancient Text reveals similar chaos for the Hebrew nation. We would do well to listen to the words of an old hymn based on Lamentations 3:

> Great is Thy faithfulness, O God my Father,
> There is no shadow of turning with Thee;
> Thou changest not, Thy compassions, they fail not;
> As Thou hast been, Thou forever wilt be.

There's the key. Somehow, on some level, we believe in a God of faithfulness. This world may not serve up much stability or peace, but there is one Source whose compassions *"fail not."*

And so we remember: God is still God, and God's hand is in the least expected places.

Places like the hospital lobby, where I witnessed a wheelchair bound grand-mother joyfully receive a six-month-old baby into her arms.

Places like the small town's school, whose senior class cancelled their senior trip in order to give the funds to a classmate newly diagnosed with cancer.

Places like the memorial service where a deceased child's dad speaks of his daughter teaching him how to love and how to die.

Chaos, though vocal, does not have the final word. Truly, God is still here.

I am an old man and
have known a great many troubles,
but most of them have never happened.

—Mark Twain

WHAT! ME WORRY?

*E*ver feel overwhelmed by what-ifs? Ever spend copious amounts of time worrying about some unforeseeable potential disaster?

Worse still, when things are going well, do you ever worry about not worrying enough (you know—waiting for the inevitable shoe to drop)? Worry is a thief that robs us of the ability to balance between two of life's tasks: dealing with harsh reality, and relishing times of pure joy.

We all know what it's like to fret, to brood, to be fearful. It's part of how we cope with our mortal limitations. In response to legitimate and not-so-legitimate threats, we worry. Some of us even worry about those who don't worry enough!

What do we worry about? You name it, we'll be obsessed with it. Finances. Family. Relationships. Purchases. Health. Church. Neighborhoods. Traffic. War. Hunger. Looks. Rejection. Moving. Strangers. Good-byes. Retirement. Enemies. Weather. Schedules. Loneliness. Ad infinitum.

Does God understand our worrying tendencies? Undoubtedly. Scriptures teem with reminders of Who is in charge, and how freeing a response of trust can be.

Check out the number of times God's appearance is accompanied by "Do not be afraid." Or Jesus rhetorically asking, "Who feeds these birds that don't sow or reap or gather into barns?" Or David's bold pronouncement: "The Lord is my light and my salvation; whom shall I fear?"

Our journey on earth seems to hinge on the quest to find the God of peace in every aspect of our lives. Crisis experiences brutally remind us: our control is limited, our dependence on a higher power is great, and our story does not end even when disaster strikes.

But as our trust grows, perhaps we begin to worry a little less. Plus with this occasional peace-giving awareness: "Lo, I am with you always even unto the end...."

I will lead the blind by ways they have not known, along unfamiliar paths. I will guide them, I will turn the darkness into light before them and make the rough places smooth. These are the things I will do; I will not forsake them.

—Isaiah 42:16

Not Yet

"I've quit trying to change everybody else. Instead, I have started listening to God's voice. I hear Him nudging me to learn to enjoy the day, even if life seems unfair."

These words came from a perky 60-ish grandmother I'll call Sarah. When she speaks, her eyes twinkle, revealing an inner spirit of playfulness and true joy.

Not that she's had an easy road to travel. She's experienced many hard knocks, each of which has taken its toll. An unwanted divorce, unpredictable teenagers, health crises of family members...these typify what she's coped with as an adult.

But Sarah's greatest grief centers around three grandchildren who live in a distant state. She's never been allowed to see the youngest, a one-year-old. Sarah's voice cracks as she relates that she has yet to see even a picture of this grandson. Sarah's efforts to bridge the communication gap with her son and his family have been met with rebuffs. She continues to send birthday greetings and gifts via mail, but she has quit trying to reach them by phone or in person.

Sarah shared with me a reminder: we have no lasting city here on earth, and the journey is never complete. Yet, she is able to find God's comfort and hope. For her, freedom comes in acknowledging the unfinished nature of this life. She finds ways not to dwell solely on the unchangeable; rather, she concedes her own limitations and responsibilities. For Sarah, God has moved beyond the walls of a church building. He has met her directly in the middle of her sorrows and joys.

Phillip Yancey's *Disappointment with God* speaks of the polarity of Hebrews 2:8. The first part of that verse triumphantly claims everything has been placed under Jesus' feet. Then comes this counterpoint: "Yet at present we do not see everything subject to him." It's as if the answer to all the unfairness of this world is summarized by "*not yet.*"

Those who deal with unhealed wounds know what it's like to wait for a better day. Chronic illnesses, shattered expectations, incomplete projects, strained relationships, unmet needs...all lead to a sense of participating in a funeral service that never ends.

Come to think of it, Sarah's story is not unlike ours. We all have our own unseen grandchildren who wait for a loving hug.

Like Sarah, we would all do well to listen to God's voice: Quit trying to change everyone else. Learn to enjoy the day, even if life seems unfair. And you will find God in these words: "Not Yet."

I was much
further out than
you thought and
not waving but
drowning.

—Stevie Smith

In the Wilderness

A PRAYER OF ONE
EXPERIENCING DEPRESSION

Lord,

At times, I feel overwhelmed.

My anxieties get the upper hand, fueled by fires of worries, of "what ifs," of "what abouts."

It bothers me, God, to have my energy sapped by an unseen, yet all-too-powerful force.

Images of darkness, of unfinished business and incomplete relationships.

Of hurts, painful encounters and rejections. Of fears of abandonment, unlovability, and worthlessness.

A quick scan of Your Word re-acquaints me with other strugglers, those whose faith and trust were not without times of despair and questioning.

People like Hagar waiting for Ishmael to die of neglect.

Like Elijah after Mt. Carmel, feeling there were no people of faith left.

Like David's challenge: "How long, O Lord, will you abandon us?"

Like Paul's thorn in the flesh.

Like Jesus' heartfelt cry in Gethsemane: "If there's any way, let this cup pass."

May such narratives touch my troubled soul, Lord.

May Your Word, Your people, Your World of sustenance remind me that it's You in charge, not me.

That this place of crisis is not the end of the story.

That Your grace, peace, and love provide ultimate hope and true joy.

I do believe, God. Help my unbelief.

Through the name of One who weeps with me,

Amen.

In the Wilderness

LESSONS FROM A HORSEBACK RIDE

In his heart a man plans his course,
but the Lord determines his steps.

—Proverbs 16:9

*M*ental cobwebs. Heavy-as-lead torso. How in the world did I wind up in this ditch? Where's Mike? Where's the horse? Why is it so quiet out here? And why am I so sore?

These were my first thoughts. Questions, actually. Questions that feebly tried to re-orient this scrambled sixth-grader's mind. Fortunately, within a few minutes, the puzzle pieces began to fit back together.

It was a gorgeous West Texas afternoon. My younger brother and I, feeling the call of after-school freedom, bridled the two horses that were a part of our farm life. Riding bareback (saddles were too much trouble, and less macho), we felt a rush of exhilaration as the horses galloped across the field. Reaching a dirt road, we slowed the horses down. They took the opportunity to come to a complete halt, eyeing some tall grass growing in the ditch.

"Cactus," the quarter horse I was riding, inched near a single wire strung along the property line. I fantasized briefly: what would it be like to touch an electric fence? But my thoughts soon returned to my horse, and I watched her long ears spring forward.

I knew why the wire was there. I assumed that Cactus was equally savvy. Like a curious cat on the prowl, she gingerly stretched her long face close to the low-humming fence. This intrigue was the last thing I remembered. My trusty steed had, in a split instant, learned the exact science of how efficiently a wet nose conducts electricity. I had, simultaneously, mastered the physics of horse-powered bodily flight.

Slowly, the jolt that blackened my consciousness wore off, and I began to reacquaint myself with reality. As I pushed myself upright with shaky arms, I spotted Cactus a half mile down the road and she was fine. My brother, I later found out, had high-tailed it to the house to inform my family that I was dead! I wasn't dead, but I was rattled, not to mention agitated. Plus, a little wiser.

It was not on my schedule for learning to take place that afternoon, but enlightenment happened. My agenda was simple: a leisurely ride to escape the confinement of a school day. Yet, that day's unscheduled tutoring is still vividly etched in my psyche and remains so decades later.

Such unscheduled, usually uninvited lessons broaden our horizons. That day I learned to expect the unexpected, to pick yourself up after being flattened, and to differentiate between assumptions and facts.

Ever been jolted by a fence-sniffing horse? Ever had some event or news totally turn your world upside down? Ever find yourself amazed that you survived, not to mention grew, because of that day?

Each of us owns a multi-dimensional storehouse garnered from the school of hard knocks. Things that disrupt, that are not in the curriculum, possess great power: power to teach new perspectives, to break preconceived notions, to reduce false conceptions of self-sufficiency. These are the spiritual and psychological nudges that can awaken our sense of the transcendent.

Life for humans is not merely physical survival. Life is a spiritual journey, one of well mapped-out highways and plenty of unplanned detours. The integration of formal education and "ah-ha" moments quickens us to hear God's calming voice. A voice that assures us that this world—and our part in it—is full of purpose and meaning.

Thanks, Lord, for letting me learn, even when I think school's out for the day.

SECTION THREE

Sharing the Trail
Being a Caregiver

Sharing the Trail
Being a Caregiver

We are, like it or not, a global community. What happens to us has a direct impact on the world around us. We can fool ourselves into believing that "it's my business only" or "no one else cares or understands," but in reality that's just not true.

Chaos can bring with it the baggage of loneliness. Disasters that befall an individual can strike fear in the hearts of fellow travelers who hope the same fate doesn't come their way. Plus, the one who endures chaotic circumstances may find all energies are directed toward putting the pieces back together, leaving little energy for reaching out to others.

But disruptions can also bring about community. Family members, neighbors, co-workers, friends, others dealing with the same disruption, even strangers are often moved to act with caring support. Those in faith communities also sense a desire to respond, believing they are called by God to identify with those who hurt or who feel like foreigners.

Call them comrades, facilitators, cheerleaders, or just caregivers: they make the unbearable bearable. They help maintain hope and perspective. They keep other parts of daily living orderly while we cope with survival.

The trail is doable with such support and love. It reflects a God who also walks all trails with us, giving us the wherewithal to endure unto completion.

Love is but the discovery
of ourselves in others,
and the delight in the recognition.

—Alexander Smith

Sharing the Trail

How Can I Thank You
for Such Teachers?

*I*n my ministry as a hospital chaplain, I have the privilege of learning a great deal about living.

I'm constantly being taught vital lessons about priorities. About real relationships. About sufferings. About hope. About the strength of sharing struggles. About not taking tomorrow for granted. About physical touch and eye contact. About the God who transcends mortal limitations. About saying "I love you."

Sometimes the fast pace of encounters with people keeps me from acknowledging such special moments. When a person leaves this world through death, I'm reminded of the unique impact that person continues to have on me.

I think of three siginifant losses which continue to mold me. These three are:

Alfredo. You were the epitome of one who would never give up. You brought real meaning to Job's statement, "Though He slay me, yet will I serve Him." You reminded me that we church members often protect ourselves from entering the world of those who are hurting. You kept finding strength through Scripture, prayer, and supportive people.

Lauren. You remained a teacher even as a hospital patient. Though only in your 20's, you had wisdom blended with enthusiasm. You knew the importance of a large, nurturing family. You refused to let illness and physical separation remove your husband and little girl from your priority list. You openly sought the counsel and prayers of others. You used your time in taking care of yourself and others.

Mark. At 17, you were a beautiful blend of childhood and adulthood. You reminded me that we all are of such a blend. You took your quiet ways to minister gently to other patients, to family, to staff, to me. You didn't let the dread of tomorrow or fear of rejection keep you from growth experiences. You taught me to grab the opportunities laid before me as gifts of God. You reminded me that expressions of affection between friends help relationships to flourish and deepen.

> *Lord God, How can I thank You for such teachers? With intense gratitude I remember these and a host of others.*
>
> *Remind me that it doesn't take the separation of death to appreciate the impact of others on my life.*
>
> *Remind me that it's often the simple, seemingly unimportant events and conversations that grow into significant memories.*
>
> *Remind us all of the insurmountable beauty and depth of Your creation, including people who are a reflection of Your everlasting love of us.*
>
> *In the name of Jesus the Teacher,*
>
> *Amen.*

Sharing the Trail

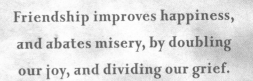

Friendship improves happiness,
and abates misery, by doubling
our joy, and dividing our grief.

—Joseph Addison

AN OPEN LETTER TO A HURTING FRIEND:
WHEN WORDS DON'T COME EASILY

My friend,

I've been touched by your current turmoil. Maybe I cannot supply instant solutions for you, so this letter is simply to remind you of our continuing friendship.

It's painfully obvious this dilemma is weighing on your heart, affecting your whole perspective right now. You are encountering experiences that disrupt, that defy any sense of fairness, that demand inordinate energy simply to cope.

I've heard "crisis" defined this way: Something of consequence which arises unexpectedly, demanding immediate attention, accompanied by intense feelings. What you are dealing with certainly qualifies as a crisis under this definition, even though you might prefer it not be labeled as such.

What you are encountering is one of those times in life that creates disorientation. It's one of those times in which, like it or not, transitions are taking place. Change, whether a welcome guest or an invading intruder, is probably the most constant companion we have. It seems that life, as we know it, seldom stands still.

I suppose, in the long run, this ongoing metamorphosis of living serves us well; yet, such growth is painful. To lose something precious, whatever it may be, is nothing short of surgery without anesthesia. Let's face it—losing hurts. And acknowledging hurt is crucial to dealing with it.

Perhaps in this area we can help each other, keeping hope rekindled by talking, listening, and accepting each other. It takes work and a level of trust to commit to such a task; yet, I firmly believe we both need such a relationship.

No doubt you're getting your share of well-intentioned platitudes, hoping to minimize pain and to focus on a hoped-for brighter tomorrow. Phrases like "Don't think about it" or "You've got to be strong for others" or "This is God's will." When you sense me trying to fix things for you in this way, please forgive me. Sometimes unanswerable questions bring about uneasy silence, and I try to fill in the gap with noise.

In short, my friend, I want you to know I care. A part of me wishes I could wave a magic wand, making all the pain disappear. I don't take your dilemma lightly, nor do I tell you lightly that my prayers and love are with you always.

Spiritual energy brings
compassion into the real world.
With compassion, we see
benevolently our own human
condition and the condition of our
fellow beings. We drop prejudice.
We withhold judgment.

—Christina Baldwin

WHEN FAMILIES WAIT

*E*arly yesterday morning, as the hospital chaplain on call, I visited the surgery waiting areas. My usual morning fog quickly dissipated as I encountered patients and families jammed into neatly arranged chairs.

All talked to me with one ear cocked, waiting to hear a specific name called. Those whose family member had already gone into surgery gave details of their loved one's plight. Eyes inadvertently welled up with tears. Some of those waiting chose not to talk at all. Many specifically asked for prayers and follow-up visits.

Some families began sharing stories with total strangers, finding solace in connecting with another family. Commonality of crises became fertile soil for a newly developing community. When I would leave the area to meet someone else, the exchange of dialogue continued unabated. Other families remained silent and chose to wait quietly.

Families and friends do lots of waiting. Waiting with, for, and on someone. If you were to write a job description of being a supportive person to a seriously ill patient, you could capture the essence in the word *waiting*.

It's one of the things we like least. We wait when we have to, but we do so begrudgingly. Waiting is a brutal reminder: we don't control everything. We cope by playing mind games, hoping the ticking seconds will pass quickly, leaving our anxious thoughts no room to take root.

Those family members and friends who wait offer a precious gift. Not every sick person has the support of involved, caring "*waiters.*" The patients who are totally alone in their recuperation present deeper challenges for medical staff mindful of the healing power of emotional as well as physical support. Hope and quality of life intensify when loving individuals surround patients.

I say this as a reminder: ministry to a patient's family and friends is ministry to that patient. Wanting to be supportive, we may find it easier to focus on the patient's world, but of equal significance is focusing on the caregiver's world. How refreshing for a tired family member to hear: "And what's your day been like?" Additionally, the proverbial cup of cold water may take the form of waiting with the patient, running errands, providing child care, or simply enjoying an unhurried cup of coffee together. Such acts rebuild, renew, and rekindle stamina.

Brianna Keisha, age 10, voiced her perceptions in a book entitled *Be a Friend: Children Who Live with HIV Speak*. Her sister, HIV positive, got sick on Thanksgiving. Brianna writes that everybody who called on the phone asking about her sister failed to ask Brianna how she was doing. She then concludes:

> *Sometimes I feel like a spirit. I feel like I can be seen but not heard. Not many people pay attention to me. Like a spirit, I am always there, but people don't notice the things I do.* ©

To those of you caring for your family member, we honor you. Forgive us for the times we make you feel like a spirit. May you know how vitally important you are to our God, to the patient, and to us.

Sharing the Trail

SOME ALTERNATIVE STATEMENTS WHEN VISITING THE SERIOUSLY ILL

When in doubt, listen.
—Lucretia Mott

"A WORD FITLY SPOKEN..."

Instead of: "I don't want to bother you with my phone calls and visits."
Try: *"Is this a good time to visit?"*

Instead of: "You've got a long, hard road ahead of you."
Try: *"No matter what happens, I want you to know you're not alone."*

Instead of: "My uncle had the same thing, and he died."
Try: *"What's going on with you today?"*

Instead of: "God knows you can handle this illness or He wouldn't have let you get it."
Try: *"In times like this, do you find your faith makes a difference?"*

Instead of:	"Don't take it personally, but I just don't like being around sick people."
Try:	*"Being with you is more important than my fear of hospitals."*
Instead of:	"Wouldn't it be better if your (husband/wife) stayed at work rather than spend so much time with you?"
Try:	*"Serious illness affects the family too, doesn't it?"*
Instead of:	"Don't worry about your job or the house. Everybody's covering for you."
Try:	*"The work is getting done, but know that you are missed."*
Instead of:	"Don't talk about dying. You're going to outlive all of us."
Try:	*"Even though it's difficult, I'm willing to talk when you are."*
Instead of:	"I'm sure God has a reason for this."
Try:	*"There's a lot in life we don't understand, isn't there?"*
Instead of:	"If there's anything I can do, let me know."
Try:	*"I am praying for you. I would also like to _____ (name specific appropriate act). What time is best for you?"*

Sharing the Trail

True silence is
the rest of the mind;
it is to the spirit
what sleep is to the body—
nourishment and refreshment.

—William Penn

IS RESTING A
WASTE OF TIME?

What's your response to this quote?

If you can spend a perfectly useless afternoon
in a perfectly useless manner,
you have learned to live.

—Lin Yutang

*D*o you, like me, tend to shoot down this concept with work-ethic logic? With heavy-handed remarks like "Go to the ant, O sluggard...A little slumber, a little folding of the hands to rest, and your poverty will come in like a vagabond" (Proverbs 6:6, 10, 11)?

Or perhaps you recall the old hymn, "Work for the Night is Coming"? Or the apostle's admonition, "If anyone will not work, neither let him eat" (2 Thessalonians 3:10 NASV).

Visitors sometimes nettle hospital patients with, "I wish I could just lie around all day." Or, "It must be nice to get a break from work and the family." Contrast this with a physician's orders to get as much rest as possible, and you've got really mixed messages!

Family members often feel such a sense of obligation to care for their sick relatives that they maintain marathon hours of caregiving. They seldom take a break to allow themselves the luxury of a good night's rest. They are reluctant to let anyone else provide support. They feel guilty if they aren't at the bedside.

Perhaps we need to look again at the biblical view of resting. After all, Creator God rested. Reflect on our Israelite heritage and see how few activities of any sort were permitted on the Sabbath. Even the land was given a seventh-year Sabbatical!

Jesus was known to pull away from the hustle of the multitudes. At times his family and closest companions were excluded. One of His compelling promises is to "Come unto me...and rest."

So what do we do—become lazy idlers? Not quite. Work accomplishments do provide satisfaction and a sense of meaning. Self-discipline that finishes a job brings gratification—to a point.

But work can become an all-consuming drive, an idol. We can rely exclusively on doing for our identity, our worth. Then other priorities of **being** lose out. God presents Himself as "*I Am*". The claim is for a Being who is capable of **doing**. In His image, we should claim no less.

If you're a hospital patient with a serious illness, allow rest to assist your healing. If you're a family member, take care of your rest needs. Then you'll have more of yourself to offer in the long haul. If you're a healthy person working away, listen to your God-given body. It will tell you when you need to rest. Trust the God of Being to get done whatever else is necessary.

Now, anyone ready for a nap?

In as much as you would
have others do unto you,
do so unto them.

—Jesus

TELL ME ABOUT IT: THE NEED TO BE HEARD

It had been a long night at the hospital. I had been working that night as the on-call chaplain. That duty consists of preoperative visits, emergency responses, and availability to family members in death situations.

The next morning, weary from the emotional strain and lack of sleep in my own bed, I called a friend to talk. In the course of that long-distance conversation regarding my previous night, he said, "Tell me about it."

These words resounded like music. They communicated loving concern and a listening ear. They assured me that my friend was interested in me more than in small talk. They lifted my spirit and gave me security. I don't remember much about my reply to my friend's invitation. I do remember his warmth in those four words: "Tell me about it."

Often each day we are given the opportunity to say, "Tell me about it." As a form of protecting ourselves, we usually respond to the tales of others with, "Let me tell you how bad I've got it." Very few of us seem interested in developing the skill that turns a conversation into a shared dialogue.

Reporting facts by telling minutely detailed boring stories is not true conversation. Instead, true conversation creates an environment that permits safe sharing of inner feelings and struggles.

George Elliot has wisely stated, "Friendship is the inexpressible comfort of feeling safe with a person, having neither to weigh thoughts or measure words." We are built in a way that yearns to share our deep feelings. We earnestly but cautiously seek out those with whom we can unmask. We inwardly cry out for someone to affirm our worth even when we don't feel worthwhile.

Look at Jesus. Looked upon as a traditional rabbinical answer-giver, he replies to hurting inquirers with gentleness. With challenges to think for oneself. With ears that listened to the whole question before answering. With a heart that saw all that the questioner could become in God's unfolding kingdom.

Look at ourselves in relating to others. Are we considered listeners or answer-givers? Do we try to fix everything that's broken? Can we leave the ending up to the individual and the Lord?

God touches the mystical and unfathomable within us. We need fellow faith-travelers to hear our experiences with that mystical, unfathomable Divinity.

Our world has plenty of people who say, "What you need to do is...." The treasured people, however, are those few who are willing to say, "Tell me about it."

A PRAYER OF ONE CARING FOR SOMEONE ILL

And call upon me
in the day of trouble;
I will deliver you,
and you will honor me.

—Psalm 50:15

Lord God,
How blessed to know You are here with me
in this place of turmoil.

My journey, Lord, is focused on
another's plight, another's needs, another's illness.
And I'm thankful that I can be here
to walk beside the one I love,
and to provide a sense of
comfort and well-being.

But God, I'm aware that this disruption
is costly, both to my loved one and to me,
leaving us both feeling out of sorts,
out of control,
like a newborn colt on wobbly legs

in a place we don't call home.

I'm mindful of others who waited, who served
    and found Your open arms and listening ears as
        a pool of refreshing water
            in a dry and thirsty place.

Faith strugglers, such as:
    The widow whose son needed Elijah's breath
    The midwife present at the birth of Jacob and Esau
    David keeping a constant vigil over his newborn
    The woman anointing Jesus' soon-to-be crucified feet
    Peter's family caring for his ill mother-in-law.

For the times I get discouraged, weary of a world
    confined to bedpans, washcloths, and injections,

I ask for Your loving intervention, Your reminders of the
    goodness of life here and beyond.

On those days when I don't even know for what to pray,
    bless me with the gentle nudges
    that whisper to do my best, and to allow
    You to do Your part.

Thank you for those family, friends, and medical staff
    who shoulder much of the weight,
    who help keep my loved one and me
        steady, focused, and affirmed.

Lord God, hear my prayer,
Give us healing, give us rest, give us life.
In the Name of the Ultimate Healer,

Amen.

SECTION FOUR

In the Valley of the Shadow
When Grief and Loss Prevail

In the Valley of the Shadow
When Grief and Loss Prevail

Death. To speak the word evokes deep sensations. Sometimes fear. Sometimes anger. Sometimes wonderment. Sometimes acceptance.

From the womb, we are created as survivors. The will to live is powerfully tenacious, a motivator stronger than despair.

As do the animal and plant kingdoms, we fight death with our inmost being. We liken death to defeat, to being overtaken by an evil enemy.

Such imagery is not unbiblical. Utopian Garden of Eden quaked at the introduction of humans tasting death. Hebrew characters spent incredible amounts of energy defending the lives of their people and themselves. The apex to the Christian narrative is a 30-plus year old carpenter's son facing death squarely in the eye, all the while promising onlookers resurrection for himself and for them. The apostle Paul refers to death as the ultimate enemy, an enemy who has been de-fanged.

We spend our lifetimes dancing with death, though not always consciously. We know that nature's life cycle depends upon the death of current residents. We acknowledge our daily bread comes at the cost of something dying on our behalf. We confront the harsh, ugly reality of death when a loved one dies, leaving us devastated and robbed.

The valley of the shadow of death is a place of loss, of bereavement, of unspeakable pain. But shadows, over time, lessen their impact as small amounts of light bring snippets of renewal.

With honest expressions of grief, with encouragement from fellow "losers," and with time, God brings us new reservoirs of faith, hope, and love.

In the Valley of the Shadow

Tears, idle tears,
I know not what they mean,
Tears from the depth of
some divine despair
Rise in the heart,
and gather to the eyes,
In looking on the
happy autumn fields,
and thinking of the days
that are no more.

—Tennyson

In the Valley of the Shadow

It Hurts to Lose:
Giving Ourselves Permission to Grieve

Janet and I spoke by long distance. It had been eight months since her 26-year old son lost his five-year battle with cancer. He died in his dad's arms at home the weekend before Christmas. Now it was August, and she spoke of the continuing adjustments to her grief. The good days and the bad days. The incredible amount of energy it took to get back to normal lifestyle functioning. She then said, "I'm learning that you can't get over this loss. You just get through it."

Losing anything precious is never easy. When something meaningful and treasured is taken from us, we grieve. It hurts to lose.

Loss and grief are not only associated with death, grief follows any significant loss. Divorce. Job lay-offs. Unfulfilled dreams. Unmet expectations. Diagnosis of serious illness. Infertility or miscarriage. Relocating. Breaking or misplacing a sentimental object. Transitions in a romance or friendship. Wrecking a car. Empty nest. Financial crisis. Retirement. Any changes of personal identity or relationship.

What are the implications for people of faith? One is the incredible commonality of pain. Every time a group gathers, loss enters the gathering. A people who meet in the Lord's name share the need to "bear one another's burdens." To be able to acknowledge one's pain, regardless of its origin, is to have one's burden lightened.

Some of us have learned well how to deny the pain of losing. Never let them see you sweat. Keep a stiff upper lip. Don't cry—it's a sign of weakness. I'll get through this just fine. Everything will work out.

Some of us have learned to dwell on nothing else but our losses. I'm a helpless victim of circumstance. Nobody really understands me. I don't want to get close to anyone. You could never understand how much I hurt.

Balanced between the two extremes of fierce independence and self-pitying helplessness is this message: *Life isn't fair*. The hopeful message from the Creator is: *Life is more than a few days of earthly existence.*

> "I come that they might have life, and have it abundantly"
> (John 10:10). We, like faith pilgrims, seek a "better country,
> that is, a heavenly one" (Hebrews 11:16 NASV).

There's more here than futuristic fantasy of the sweet bye-and-bye of heaven. There's a message of affirming, not denying, the pain of losing precious treasures. There's a message that shared tears allow emotions to be aired and deep love to flourish. There's a message that, even if we feel we've been abandoned, God is indeed with us. There's a message that the pain of losing someone precious is a barometer for how much that person, even though gone, continues to nourish us.

Lord, may we acknowledge our pain, feel our losses, keep our perspective that transcends the pain, and be willing to enter the pain of fellow travelers. In the name of the One who shares our grief. Amen.

The opposite of talking
isn't listening.
The opposite of talking
is waiting.

—Fran Lebowitz

SOME ALTERNATIVE STATEMENTS
WHEN CONFRONTING THE CRISIS OF GRIEF

Instead of: "I know exactly how you feel."
Try: *"I can only imagine what you are going through."*

Instead of: "At least he doesn't have to suffer anymore."
Try: *"He suffered through a lot, didn't he?"*

Instead of: "It's God's will."
Try: *"One comfort I find is God's promise never to abandon us."*

Instead of: "Take this pill—it will calm you down."
Try: *"Do you feel like talking right now?"*

Instead of: "She wouldn't want you to grieve."
Try: *"It's hard to say goodbye, isn't it?"*

Instead of: "Don't cry—you'll only make it worse."
Try: *"Sometimes tears are the best way to express our feelings."*

Instead of: "This death is a great victory for God."
Try: *"Even with the promise of resurrection, it hurts to give someone up."*

Instead of: "You can't be angry with God."
Try: *"God understands even when we're upset."*

Instead of: "At least you have other family members."

Try: *"There's no way to replace the one you've lost, is there?"*

Instead of: "Don't you think it's time to get on with living your life?"

Try: *"Everyone has to grieve in their own way, don't they?"*

Instead of: "Don't talk about the funeral—it'll only make you sad."

Try: *"We can talk about whatever you want."*

Instead of: "Time heals all wounds."

Try: *"Time will lessen the pain, but you'll always have a part of him/her with you."*

Instead of: "You've got to be strong."

Try: *"I want you to know it's okay to be yourself around me."*

In the Valley of the Shadow

FOR DAVID (1973–1992)

He's gone, Lord.
At least as far as his body goes.
The ten years of leukemia. Remissions and recurrences.
The suffering, the rally, the waiting—ended Tuesday.

Yet, he's still so much here.
The pictures—the endless conversations—the funeral—the memorial
service. But, mostly, it's my heart that rebels—it cries out—he can't be gone.
Not now. Not this time. He'll come back. He'll call. He'll squeeze my hand.

He won't, will he Lord?
Before, I could see him respond a little, then a lot. Now none.
No warmth, no opening eyes, no tear, no breath.

I can't fathom it, God.
Sure, it's an obsolete body, a used up entity, an empty shell.
But he's always come back before.
Even with the odds against him this time, I wanted to believe.

He's still touching my life, Lord.
So many ways, with such depth and honesty.
With caring eyes and a gentle voice.
With his energetic smile and sorrow-filled tears.

Take care of him. Please. He deserves to rest.
Shelter him. Allow him total freedom. Bathe him in the sunlight of Your face.
You, the God who shared him with me, I thank.

Disrupted

Never will I leave you,
never will I forsake you.

—Hebrews 13:5

In the Valley of the Shadow

REMEMBRANCE

*L*ord, God, Creator of life...temporal and eternal...

Hear our prayer of remembrance.

Our lives have been touched in multiple layers
By those who have left us, crossing through the valley of death
Into the world beyond.

Some have gone recently, our hearts raw with pain.
Some departed years ago, yet they transcend time and touch our souls again.

To You, our Maker, we acknowledge our grief lessened in intensity over time.
Yet still, the gap, the absence haunts us
And we find ourselves missing them, and desiring reunion.

In moments of remembrance like these
We also, with grateful hearts, offer thanks
    for lives that continue
    to touch us deeply
    to remind us of our incompleteness and
    to teach us about hope
And about You, whose name is Love.

Amen.

One doesn't discover new lands
without consenting to lose sight
of the shore for a very long time.

—Andre Gide

In the Valley of the Shadow

THE ONLY WAY OUT IS THROUGH

*I*n hearing about sorrowful events from hurting people, a fellow-chaplain often responds: "The only way out is through." Truth is sometimes painful. Reality of losses can be masked and suppressed for a time, but, the pain, fear, doubts and inner struggles still exist.

We Americans live in a death-denying culture. Youth is extolled over age. Physical prowess, wealth and power determine worth. It's okay to hurt briefly if a gain (fitness, prestige) can be realized. It's not okay to hurt (at least publicly) over losses from sickness, divorce, or brokenness.

Consider the Oklahoma City bombing, or 9/11, or Virginia Tech. Almost immediately television commentators and stunned townspeople were trying to ask why such a tragedy occurred. Speculations were offered: "Perhaps it's God's will." "Perhaps something good will come out of this." "Perhaps we all needed reminding of how fragile human life is." "Perhaps we'll never understand."

As television cameras zoomed into grief-stricken faces, we all joined in chorus, "Why?" And, "Why them and not us?" And, "Let's see some pictures of people getting back to living." Or, "Let's have a happy ending to this story."

Grief counselors know it takes months and years for family members and friends to process their grief, to reconcile themselves to permanent separation, to find hope and peace and comfort in daily living. Yet the camera crews are gone. Only scattered news columns update us on these tragedies. Implied is that the rest of the world can safely assume that all grievers are fine, that they're adjusting, that they're not hurting anymore. We assume that no news is good news.

Somehow the church has a message here. Not of easy answers to unanswerable questions of why. Not of insisting everyone keep smiling because God is in control. Not of hoping the hurt will not be around long enough to disturb us.

No, the message of the church is in her Bible, a sacred text chock-full of laments and celebrations. Creation and re-creation. The futility and the hopefulness of humanity. Powers of evil and righteousness. Mortality and everlasting life. The pain of failure and the joy of grace. The gardens of Eden and Gethsemane. Calvary and the borrowed empty tomb.

The true Gospel message is this: God has cared, is caring, and will always care. God loves. God comforts. God hears. God is.

The implication for us is this: No one hurts alone. We can admit our pain without fearing rejection. We can allow ourselves time to share memories, distress, and turmoil. We can cling to the assurance that there's more to life than what we experience here. We can remember that brokenness, sickness, evil, and death all sting—but they don't have to have the final word.

Indeed, the only way out is through.

**The heart has its reasons
which reason knows nothing of.**

—Blaise Pascal

In the Valley of the Shadow

A Prayer of One Experiencing Loss

Lord God,
> Giver of life
> Source of all that exists
Hear my prayer of pain.

My life is in shambles for
The one I love dearly is gone.
Removed from my world
Yanked from my heart.

Often I wonder, Lord
> Am I crazy?
> Am I selfish?
> Am I unfaithful?

Often I question, Lord
> Are You aware?
> Are You responsible?
> Are You there?

Yet, in the midst of dark moments
Flickers of renewed energy spark my soul.

Memories that bring tears sometimes bring
    unexpected smiles.
My broken heart remembers:
    You are not a distant god, but rather,
    You are God—revealed as One
    who knows grief firsthand.

Lord, I beg for Your assured presence.
For those who
    share my grief
    and allow me to be me,
    I thank You.
For having my heart touched
    by the love of the one now gone,
    I thank You.

May Your gentle arms of comfort
    soothe my aching spirit.
May Your name—I AM—
    be victoriously proclaimed,
    even in the valley of death.

  Amen

Disrupted

SECTION FIVE

Green Pastures

Times of Reflection and

Thanksgiving

Green Pastures
Times of Reflection and Thanksgiving

$\mathcal{S}$piritual journeys traverse multi-faceted arenas. Stormy seas, wilderness and deserts, rocky trails, and shadow-engulfed valleys take their toll. Stagnation and boredom stand no chance in such environments.

As a counterbalance, life journeys also supply stations of refreshment and renewal. Like irrigated green pastures in the middle of the desert terrain, spirituality offers the occasional respite. Spending time on emotional mountaintops or in lush pastureland gives us a spark—a sense of

Disrupted

reconnecting with the Ultimate Power. God's loving presence becomes clearer, more evident, in such times.

The creation story in Genesis ends each day's progression with this affirmation: And It Was Good. We are invited into the Creator's mind and heart, which relished goodness, cohesive cooperation, and rest.

Likewise, we know reflective moments that reaffirm the basic goodness of this world. And the joy of seeing nature and humanity working as partners. And the blissful refreshment that a good night's rest brings after a tiring day.

It's not always easy or possible to experience green pastures. The journey takes too many unforeseen turns to allow us to coast totally carefree. But sometimes, when we least expect it, God's voice breaks through our chaos and gently reminds us: "I am God, and you are mine. Enjoy the day, even in the middle of your turmoil. For I am with you, and I have overcome the world."

Such news is nothing short of a priceless gift. One to be unwrapped on mountains, valleys, and places in-between.

Teach me to listen, Lord,
when You speak in whispers.

—Lois T. Henderson

HAVE A NICE JOURNEY

It was a typical, somewhat rushed day for me. My intended schedule included getting some visits made in the hospital. But I was running behind. Too many interruptions and self-induced distractions had me feeling hurried and harried. Loaded with impatience, I scurried to recoup time lost to other endeavors.

Getting on the elevator, I pushed the button for floor number 7. Another man accompanied me, but I paid little attention to him. Without fanfare, the elevator doors opened on the seventh floor. As I began to exit, the man cheerily exhorted me: "Have a nice journey." The doors closed behind me. He and the elevator moved on.

I wanted to seek him out and thank him, except that was impossible. Not only was he gone, he was unidentifiable, for I had not seen his face.

Maybe it was the gracious tone of his voice, or the unexpected jolt to my jumbled thoughts, or the gentleness of the words. Regardless, it was a wonderfully interrupting message of grace. His simple words cascaded refreshment to this frazzled chaplain.

My perceptual lenses were suddenly re-focused in that instant. This anonymous friend had brought me a better perspective, a lift to my spirit, a sound-bite phrase of renewal. All packaged and delivered in a split second.

His message reminded me of Henri-Frederic Amiel's observation: *Kindness is gladdening the hearts of those who are traveling the dark journey with us.*

Or this slice of discernment from Proverbs 25:11:

A word aptly spoken is like apples of gold in settings of silver.

The world we humans occupy is certainly rife with discord, sown by all of us when we are at our self-serving, myopic worst. "Where seldom is heard a discouraging word" can seldom be said about most of us.

And yet, conversely, how powerful are those wisp-like moments when courtesy and genuine well-wishing abound. And how grateful I am to be the undeserving recipient of one who unashamedly shared his blessing of kindness.

Now if you'll excuse me, I have some work to enjoy.

Disrupted

Green Pastures

THROUGH THE YEARS

There is no such thing as the pursuit of happiness,
but there is the discovery of joy.

—Joyce Grenfell

Lord God,

When our calendar runs out of pages
and the months dissipate into December,
it's easy to be surprised, even disbelieving,
that another year is closing.

That, in the hurriedness of living life,
the sands of time have continued unfettered,
and we are forced to close a chapter
in order to move on and grow.

Such a process isn't easy, for we're not
good at saying goodbye.

With a sense of wonder and a twinge of sadness,
we reflect upon the experiences of the sweeping years.

We see vividly through memory's prism
friends, family, others, from distant past and
within-touch present,
each of whom has touched and shaped us,
each of whom is unique
yet so very much like us.
For every friendship, we give thanks.

For those from whom we are distanced through miles,
we pray for their well-being.
For those from whom we are distanced through death,
we pray for the ongoing gift of recall.

As our journey continues,
we trust in Your promised presence.
We are grateful for the companionship You offer
in the form of fellow travelers
who teach, enrich, share joy, and dry tears.

As the years unfold, Lord, we stop and thank You
for the truth that You are love.
And as new years unfurl, may we always find
You along the way.

Amen.

Disrupted

And God smiled again,
and the rainbow appeared,
and curled itself
around his shoulder.

—James Weldon Johnson

A PRAYER OF REFLECTION
AND THANKSGIVING

Lord God,
    Creator and Sustainer of life—
life too vast to comprehend
life too microscopic to behold.
Life of spirit, flesh, soul and mind,
    all intrinsically woven
    by Your love-filled hands.

We marvel at Your universe,
    its unfathomable expansiveness
    its power to replenish and to nurture.
We consider our place in the created order,
    sometimes with questions of anguish and pain
    sometimes with arrogant pride
    sometimes with child-like wonder and thanksgiving.

Our vision, clouded and nearsighted, often
    fails to see Your handiwork,
    Your ongoing re-creation,
    Your voice that breaks through chaos.

Instead we focus on unfairness, on unmet expectations,
　　　on mortal limitations and natural disasters,
　　　on differing perceptions and disagreements.

And yet, still at certain
　　　sacred moments
　　　the clouds break
And You stand in clear vision,
　　　embracing us, showing us purpose
　　　and meaning,
　　　reminding us we are Your children.

For those moments, we are truly grateful.

At those times we are touched by You
　　　through another's kindness,
　　　honest conversations,
　　　and genuine acceptance.

Lord God,
Creator and Sustainer
　　　of life,

We give thanks.

Each portion, properly completed, leads naturally into another.

—Anonymous

"Oh, Grow Up!"

We adults must appear strange to children. We've got fully developed bodies and capable minds to master many tasks. We drive cars, buy and sell real estate, vote, change careers, get married and stay up late. Children can't wait to get old enough to do all these things.

But there are other sides to adult behavior that seem much closer to childishness than maturity. Go to a Little League baseball game and try to figure out for whom the game is really being played. Watch two grown men on the freeway weave back and forth trying to outwit each other in revenge tactics. Listen to reasons divorcing people list as grounds for dissolving a marriage. Ask church leaders how often they are threatened with "do it my way or I'll attend elsewhere."

I imagine there are times when our children could shout to us: "Why don't you just grow up!" There are times when we look in the mirror and say that very thing to ourselves.

One of the central messages of the Bible is this complexity: We humans share individual uniqueness and unquestionable similarities. I must remember that there is only one *me*; I must also remember that I'm not so unique that I don't share the essence of humanity. Finding a healthy balance between these two brings us directly to God. God as Creator. Provider. Reconciler. Savior. Nurturer. Judge. God in all things—spiritual and temporal.

As the reinstated Peter heard Jesus predict the future events of Peter's life, he quickly pointed to John and asked, "Lord, what about him?" Jesus' terse reply: "What is that to you? You must follow me" (John 21:22). A modern paraphrase might be, "Paddle your own canoe—let John and me worry about his role."

Frequently we adults spend great amounts of energy focusing on other people's business. We can easily delineate the blame that another person has in our own failures. We hope that by saying "what about him or them," the spotlight will shine elsewhere.

Maturity stops spending so much wasted time on laying blame. Maturity says, "I blew it." Maturity lessens bragging and increases honest vulnerability. Maturity acknowledges that conversion and regeneration are daily processes, not once-for-all steps. Maturity doesn't demand someone else to do for me what I should be doing myself. Maturity avoids the extreme of self-flagellation ("I can't do anything right"). Maturity permits us to pray openly, to accept imperfections in others, and to laugh at ourselves. Instead of "what about him," maturity asks, "what about me?"

Are we ever fully mature? Not in this lifetime. We are, however, always maturing.

The next time you tell yourself, "Oh, grow up," reply this way: "With God's grace and with God's timing, I am growing up."

There is more to life than
increasing its speed.

—Mahatma Gandhi

Green Pastures

GOOD THINGS / BEST THINGS

Don't let the good things of life
rob you of the best things.

—Malthie D. Babcock

GOOD THINGS	BEST THINGS
Stereo system	Music of the soul
Luxury car	Freedom to maneuver
House	Home
Bible study	Relationship with God
Numbers of acquaintances	True friends
Health	Living abundantly
Memories	Today nurtured by yesterday, hopeful of tomorrow
Employment	Fulfillment
Money	Ability to have and to share
Vacations	Relaxation, refreshment
Spouse	Soul mate
Painless death	Dying with dignity
Compliments	Honest appraisal, unconditional acceptance
Spontaneity	A trusting, child-like spirit
Survival, longevity	Meaningful, purposeful living

Knowledge	Wisdom and love
Winning	Learning, enjoying, respecting
Hearing	Listening
Quiet	Contemplative silence
Seeing	Absorbing truth and beauty
Membership	Belonging, inclusion
Words	Heartfelt communication
Desires and goals	Gratitude and a sense of being
Dreaming of the exotic	Appreciating miraculous simplicity
Forgiveness	Reconciliation
Happiness	Peace and joy

I have come that they may have life,

and have it to the full.

—Jesus of Nazareth

The glory of friendship is not the outstretched hand, nor the kindly smile nor the joy of companionship, it is the spiritual inspiration that comes to one when he discovers that someone else believes in him and is willing to trust him.

—Ralph Waldo Emerson

Disrupted

Green Pastures

WITH THANKSGIVING FOR FRIENDSHIPS

Lord God,
I stand in awe
of the rejuvenating power of friendships.
With welcoming warmth, You have breathed
into the very fiber of my soul
The need for others
The drive to connect
The will to belong.

Your Word is clear: we need each other.
As with Adam, "this is bone of my bones,"
As with the Preacher, "two are stronger than one,"
As with Jesus, "where two or more are gathered,"
As with Paul, "be given to hospitality."

It's hard work, Lord,
to be in relationships.
At times, I seek solitude
far from the maddening crowd
hoping to alleviate the pain of
misunderstanding and brokenness.
But then, I am reminded that I cannot
survive alone, nor drink of life's deepest waters,
in total isolation.

And so I return to the fray of humanity,
asking and giving words of
forgiveness and reconciliation.
And again run the risk of investing in people,
knowing that it costs dearly.

Thank You, Lord,
for those who befriend me
who give me gentle nudges, engaging eyes,
    listening ears, and warm hands.
Who remind me that at the fiber of Your Essence,
You are revealed as
A God of gentle nudges, engaging eyes,
    listening ears, and warm hands.

Amen.

Disrupted

Green Pastures

MOUNTAINS, VALLEYS, & PLACES IN-BETWEEN

Even God lends a hand to honest boldness.

—Menander

Elijah replied, "Now summon the people from all over Israel to meet me on Mount Carmel"...when all the people saw this, they fell prostrate and cried, "The Lord—He is God!"

Then Elijah was afraid and ran for his life, and went a day's journey into the desert. He came to a broom tree, sat down under it, and prayed that he might die.
(1 Kings 18:19,39; 19:3,4)

Dear Lord,
Those of us journeying through this world
Find the terrain ever-changing,
Complete with high and low spots, and
Lots of places in-between.

We enjoy the mountain-top experiences,
Those rare serendipitous moments when
Your powerful, loving presence is confirmed
In resounding, undeniable ways.
Such celebratory moments as:
 enjoying a significant friendship

welcoming a child into the family
arriving home after a long hospitalization
finishing a long-term project
worshipping You with heart-felt gratitude.

Yet, like Elijah following Mount Carmel's triumph,
We often are caught in the emotional abyss
Of seeming defeats, fear, and feelings of worthlessness
And find ourselves sitting under a broom tree
Waiting, even asking for, a hurried ending to the misery.
Such despondent moments as:
yearning for a friend's company, but not getting it
losing a child through miscarriage, moving out, or death
being denied the chance to go home
seeing a string of well-intentioned, yet unfinished projects
worshipping You while inwardly struggling with unclear messages.

Lord, it seems as if highs and lows, mountains and valleys, are
part and parcel of our spiritual quest.
We ask for, and need, Your loving mercy
During the times of jubilant celebration
The times of wilderness wanderings
And all the times in-between, when
Daily living and mundane decisions dominate us.

We thank You for preserving the Elijah story,
And for reminding us, You are indeed God
Of Mount Carmel, Mount Horeb, and places in-between.

Amen.

Disrupted

Notes

Pg. 16   "The Rime of the Ancient Mariner" by Samuel Taylor Coleridge
            (1772–1834).

Pg. 43-44   "I'm a Little Cookie" by Larry Penn, Copyright © 1978 & 1984,
            Devon Music, Inc., New York, New York. Used by permission.

Pg. 52   "Great Is Thy Faithfulness" words by Thomas O. Chisholm,
            Copyright © Hope Publishing Co. Used by permission.

Pg. 58   *Disappointment with God: Three Questions No One Asks Aloud* by
            Philip Yancy, Grand Rapids, Zondervan Publishing House, 1997.

Pg. 76   *Be a Friend: Children with HIV Speak,* edited by Lori S. Weiner.
            Albert Whitman and Co., 1994.

A COMPANION VOLUME BY THE SAME AUTHOR

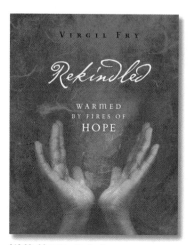